Face *in the* Window

CHERYL KNOLL

Printed in the United States of America

ISBN 979-8-89114-030-1 (sc)
ISBN 979-8-89114-031-8 (hc)
ISBN 979-8-89114-032-5 (e)

Library of Congress Control Number: 2023922588

2024.01.17

MainSpring Books
5901 W. Century Blvd
Suite 750
Los Angeles, CA, US, 90045

www.mainspringbooks.com

Contents

Face in the Window

A face in the window, looking out
It looked for something to write about
A reason to write, to write to live
The face searched God for something to give
For years she looked out, many nights many days
The window she looked out went both ways
For God so loves the faces that seek
And search for His hands that hold it all
The face in the window looked up to God
The face had ears that heard the call

The Window Opened

The window opened
I just stared
I felt the wrath God wanted aired
There's something to say
And feelings to feel
Warnings he made known as real
My ears opened
My pen repeated
What God wanted, till it was completed
He showed my pen the words to speak
Words for the strong to help the weak
Stand strong, give fear no place to rest
Watch as I stir the evil nest
Feel no fear and enjoy the show
They will see my wrath! They will know
They will know!
I wrote what I saw
Till the feelings let go

God's Fury

His fury sparked, then fanned it flamed
It made a list with the traitors named
Treason, betrayal, greed and more
God has a plan and it hit the floor

Hey you!
You're wearing black leotards roaming the street
You find innocent people to attack, stab and beat
Run you little cowards, many to one
Put on your glasses or you'll miss the fun
God has a plan you cannot control
It was your own shovel, you dug your hole

There are colleges filled with Marxist professors
Professing nonsense, America's traitors
Your children are brainwashed, now socialist prey
The socialist alligators, dragging them away
Then there's you
Now, a shameful organization, spouting a mantra
You have chosen one race, but to God all lives matter
Working to destruct the law we deserve
Demonizing the strong who protect us and serve
God says you are a racist monster inside
Lay your shameful signs down, and pick up your pride

Now you politicians, woe! Woe, woe!
Where in the hell did your morals go?
You solicit and beg for money, even from the poor
God looks and sees you're a money whore
You are supposed to be representing your states
You beg folks for money on your way to hell's gates
There are good politicians, though they are very few
You better go join them, God's wrath will soon spew

The fury that sparked, then fanned, it flamed
Is now in the process of burning those named
Stealing elections, accusing the innocent of lying
That is only going to make the fire hotter for frying

To one more group God has something to say
They are getting on his nerves and these words gave way

You are a small group, but you yell with loud voices
You want everyone to accept your sexual choices
You shove it down people's throats! Yes, you do!
Well, keep it to yourself because they want to spew
Most of this country lives life their own way
They don't put their sex out on banners to display
Your sexual preferences make their heads ache
Just go live your own life and give them a break

God sees many people are becoming disgraces
He can barely stand to look at some faces
They turn their backs on him going their own way
Yet, he will always have mercy, if they will come back and pray
Sin separates people from God
Sometimes He has no choice but to correct with a strong rod

Calling All Fathers

The face opened the window, the ears heard a sound
Where are the fathers? Why aren't they around?
God's wrath was sounding and shaking my head
He's angered by some men and here's what he said

You had your way, she didn't say no
You both created life and your seed did grow

You didn't stay and reap your reward
Your child grew up as someone else's ward
My love for you is disseminating
Because you are not fathering your inseminating
Just look around and see families decline
That was your choice! It was not mine!
You were supposed to raise them in the way they must go
Only you shirked your duties! You're the one who said no!

Children need fathers, that was my plan
Why don't you take on your responsibilities as a man!
If you don't want children, then don't perform the act
My children are suffering from the fathers they lacked

Now stand up and be fathers and get back to work
Then I'll stop calling you an incompetent jerk

Wrong Path

The lies are flying as moral are falling
The leaders we voted for lost their calling
Some elected leaders put God's book away
They're on the wide path and they do not pray
They're drinking in power and burping up lies
On their path to destruction and their own demise
For wide is the path
Where many will go
And it leads to hell, so
They better walk slow

Rat Trapper

Funny music played as the sneaky rat danced
The rat trapper has his eye on you
You're nestled in lies behind the scene
But the rat trapper is very keen

Everyone wonders where the rat is?
We can sure smell him
He's leaving droppings
The traps are set, and his snout needs chopping

He has a network of tunnels and holes
He's been engaging other rats and moles
He has our governing bodies infested
He almost has China fully invested

The agents who trap rats are only trapping bunnies
They like the rats for all their monies
Now a new rat trapper came to town
He knows how to take the rat down

The sneaky rat has a hidden agenda
He thinks he's in charge behind the scene
There's only one thing he keeps forgetting
The rat trapper is very keen

The enterprising Trump Company crafted a new trap
It's hiding in a red hat and has a powerful snap
You should see this hat and its hidden power
Rats are being caught, living their last hour

No more sneaky rats behind the scene
I told you the rat trapper was very keen

Selling California

The face in the window, looked out one night
The sight was terrifying, a horrible site
Downtown California as if a dam broke
Water eighty feet high, no it wasn't a joke

Buildings were crashing and flooding away
I wasn't there but I saw God's display
His fury was flooding, knocking everything down
God is disappointed, California turn around

Oh California, how could it be
You banned me and canned me and now you can't see
Your cities once jewels filled with sunshine life
Now your streets wear feces and homeless and strife

God's back is turning and now his face you won't see
Your leaders are disgraces, and your state isn't free
They've ruined your cities and sold out your state
To communist Marxists all the way to hell's gate

Your leaders are snakes, they don't speak, they hiss
I've turned my blessings off, and I'll tell you this
I have no pity for the homeless on your streets
The drug infested lazy suckling government teats
Your leaders rake in money sitting on their lazy seats
The few who truly need help, your kind of help defeats

California, California, you're not cool anymore
Your leaders sold you out like a pimp and a whore
You're hanging in the balance and soon you'll hang no more
Get rid of your disgusting leaders and bend your knees to the floor
Pray for forgiveness, pray for mercy, pray to me
Pray or you may well cease to be

My Godly and righteous ones, living in your state
My hand will protect them all the way to my gate
My people I love deserve better than this
Crooked leaders, feces, homeless and piss

Just my rare treasures left in this once golden land
Hold on my beloved, keep hold of my hand

God's righteous people will stand up for him there
Don't forget what God said, crooked leaders beware

The Vote

We studied the tickets, our votes were cast
We were the sideshow, their act didn't last
Like a carnival ride, they spun us around
The ride went up, the ride came down
They promised us some junk
Some carnival food
They said they were for us
Our votes they wooed
The show is over, the carnival done
They lied again after our votes were won
They promised us corndogs and funnel cakes
They returned our votes with frogs and snakes

The Plan

Appalling evil falls
Fallen angels with balls
Spiritual death calls
As they enter your walls

Next hear the wails
As evil prevails
Every effort fails
As Satan, earth hails

A time or two
Believers dwindle to few
Jesus is due
To salvage his few

No more veil
Truth will prevail
Christ we will hail
As he chops Satan's tail

Invisible Giant

The face looked out the window, everything looked still
Though outside were voices that caused a great chill
A hidden evilness, America deceived
There is not a race problem as you have believed
It's a façade, it is just not true
There's a giant you can't see, doing this to you
This giant is evil and causing disorder
Created to blind you to a new rising order
America loves races and gives them her best
The giant is deceitful and causing unrest
You can't see the truth right in front of your eyes
A voice told my ears as God opened my eyes
Keep them distracted while billionaires pay
To change America's power, they are well on their way
God is spewing fury. His wrath burns like fire
Put the giant to death and make racism retire
The giant, the socialist, communist rule
End it and kill it, end racism's fuel
God's anger thundered, you listen well
He's had it with this evil giant
He's had it with the lies
Evil billionaires created it and it's a disguise
Put the racist giant to bed
Gouge out its eyes and chop off its head

America's Heartbeat

America's heart is her free and the brave
Not the cowardly socialist slave
Her blood that flows red, white and blue
Stands strong for the blood once shed for you
Her heartbeat thunders loudly, loudly
We stand up for America proudly
Enemies living upon her land
Cannot be heirs, their shame will stand
Her heartbeat thunders loudly, loudly
Her patriots stand for America proudly

Bad News, Bad Views

To the mainstream media I will not bow
The words you speak are like slop for a sow
Like vomit for a dog to eat
You won't find me suckling your fake news sow teat
You stir your words into big lie pies
Here's a big slice, have another slice of lies
Your pies are rotten, and they attract flies
The flies are the hosts, regurgitating their pies
You think your viewers believe your lies are true
You don't give people credit for being smarter than you
The more you lie, the more your lips stretch
I refuse to listen, or I would sure retch
The owners of fake news networks are USA traitors
They are communist lovers and America haters
And your views, clean your glasses, you really should
From where you're keeping your heads
You're not seeing very good
Your lies and bastardly distortions you choose
All I can say is bad news, bad views

God's Babies

The face in the window stood there looking
The ears on the face heard the crying
The music was crying, and eyes were crying
Everything was crying as babies were dying
The music played and it tore at my heart
They're tearing my babies, my babies apart
They're killing my babies still in the womb
Womb to tomb! Womb to tomb!
They're killing my babies I put in the womb

The tears welled up and the wrath of God poured
They're pulling my babies out, spinal cords gored
My babies are kicking and writhing in pain
They're killing my babies again and again
Utter contempt I have for your killing
Doctor killers, your killing is willing
Wait till you see what's in store for you
I sent this message and soon you'll be through

Mothers that kill my babies in the womb
That is not your right and punishment will loom
For killing my babies still in the womb
My babies, my babies, I put in the womb

Blood to Mud

Another evil giant standing on our land
A blood red letter D, for death it does stand
Planning deaths for fetuses, it's going down
In murdered embryonic fluid it's going to drown
The blood of the innocent has brought God's full wrath
He's going to wash it in its own blood bath
The bigger they are the harder they go down
The whole world is going to feel this giant hit the ground

They won't be a murdering organization anymore
I watched three bloody letters walk out their door
They formed themselves out of all the innocent blood
They put themselves together and the word spelled mud
They were M... U. D, and I thought I was being toyed
Then those three letters formed their own words
Murderers Utterly Destroyed

Praise be to God and his holy name
He's going to give them a heaping of shame
He's going to rip them out of their protected room
Once again, God's babies will live full term in the womb

No more of these lies that this killing is good
This giant is going to wear the executioner's hood

The Spear Tip Stings

Chosen by God long ago
He found a man to call upon
To lead our America, he so loves
Back to greatness as in its dawn

God eyed a man and with guided hand
Found a great leader after his own heart
He could stand up for God without fear
He had a faithfulness that would not part

Before this man, the leaders of our nation
Took us on a perilous course
They worked to bring in a new world order
They were evil men with no remorse

With veiled plans to implement
Piece by piece a dismantling
Of the greatest country inspired by God
Those leaders will now feel the sting

Installed now by the hand of God
The man God chose to right the course
He will bring retribution to our traitors
And all their treason with our military's force

America's president, chosen by God
He will fight and do what's right in God's eyes
Who would have thought our own past leaders
Would deliberately work to our nation's demise

Beware of God's Trump, the spear tip stings
That's what selling off America brings

Satan's Parade

The face in the window could only stare
Wondering what those people were doing out there
The face saw parades of people in trances
Leading the procession, Satan laughing as he dances
Satan stepping high, with a shit eating grin
Helping to march the illegal ones in
Wealthy cartels are laughing all the way
To make sure America will soon go away

Our borders are wide open
Despicable to say the least
It's the raping of America
By a government beast

They are raping our borders to get money and houses
Filled credit cards, free groceries, our government douses
While hard working citizens struggle and work
The government says" pay more taxes you jerk"
Someone must pay the non-citizens way
The corrupt ones want real citizens to pay

The government now, a monstrosity of greed
Their jaws flapping lies for yet another dirty deed
This country, once powerful, free and strong
Is being raped by those who do not belong

A storm is brewing, the citizens will rise
They'll have a big mess to clean when the parade dies
The face saw the parades were turning about
American patriots with guns pointing
to show the way out

The Hidden Fight

Smoke screens, mirrors, deceitful visions
Don't believe what you hear and see
The evil underworld is going down
The painful truth will set you free
Murdering children for Adrenochrome
Satanism is alive and well
God has evil in a choke hold
His army is sending them to hell
The curtain is rising on deceit
You're going to see a painful show
You'll watch while squirming in your seat
You'll say dear God! I did not know

Crazy Times

Night is falling to its eminent domain
Sleep, a welcome reprieve for the sane
Days more troubling than the night
Hell on earth and sin like blight
Righteousness calls for a fight
The gloves are off, they got too tight
Hands now swell to take on hell
Forgive me Lord
Profanity I may yell

God's Agenda, Not Satan's

To my fellow Americans who have had enough
With the gender agenda and its corrective stuff
I will never adhere to their lunacy rules
If you're able to fight, get it out of our schools
Those children will be running our country someday
We don't want it run by nerves that will fray
God always was and he will always be
He made us male and female, he made us he and she
God's word said we were intricately created
We weren't born confused or other gender fated
You are letting your children be taught lies
The gender agenda is satanism in disguise

Satan has been destroying the family from the beginning
It's time for us to fight this, we need God's agenda winning

The Evil Encounters

The face couldn't look out the window that night
Something felt creepy, something wasn't right
The face would not look, so the vision came in
The face had to watch fallen angels in their sin
The face's body was chilled to the bone
When it saw those who didn't know Jesus Christ on the throne
Satan and the fallen angels fell like stars
They were loosed and thrown out from God's chains and bars
The vile sights now seen, barely believed
For the angels were so handsome and people were deceived
The lonely and sexual couldn't resist
The seduction, when the handsome ones did insist
While the unbelievers were being abused and seduced
The fallen angels laughed, that they had been let loose
After the encounters, people felt pain and remorse
Yes, they fell for the fallen angel's passion with force
After those horrible sights of those abused
The face was not well and said, "may I be excused?"
A glass of wine and a couple of (all natural) sleeping pills
And knowing it was from God, helped ease the ills
The face did not take pharmaceutical sleeping pills

Light the Match Please

Congress is a tinder box full of dry wood
It's piled so high; it's going to burn good
God has the match for the rotten wood piled high
He's going to burn it as the just folks stand by
When the ashes are removed, the floor once again cleaned
The just ones will rebuild with new wood that was gleaned
We will build a new house with only truth spoken
The old house was evil, and our trust was broken
Congress is going to be tried by God's fire
Watch me laugh as the flames go higher
Bring down this congress and all the dry wood
God's truth is the match, and it's going to burn good

Justice For the Innocent

Death is the only acceptable penalty
For the hideous crime of child raping
The electric chair can fry those to vapors
Make no mistake, for God's wrath's no escaping
The firing squad would be getting off easy
They deserve hanging or frying in the chair
They need to be executed and sent to God's judgement
Then child raping would be rare

College Professors

The face in the window went for a look
The face jumped when nearly smacked by a book
The spinning and twirling and trying to stand upright
What the face saw was a confounding sight
The college professors were all wearing dunce caps
Their classes were filled with rabbits and dogs
They were trying to teach the rabbits to be squirrels
They were trying to teach the dogs to be frogs
The dogs chased the rabbits in their gender confusion
Knocking down the professors, giving each a contusion
The dogs that thought they were frogs
And the rabbits who thought they were squirrels
Were confused as to whether they were boys or girls
After so much confusing discussion
Every professor had received a concussion
The confused ones sitting there coloring faces
Were scared to pick colors as not to offend races
All the while antifa was bashing out windows
And beating the dogs and the rabbits and confused
Parents, don't send your kids to radical colleges
Your hard-earned money will be wasted and abused
The good professors God was holding in his hand
Were grateful they weren't teaching
In the radical's folly land

The Lesson

The face in the window took a glance out
Took another longer look
What was that all about?
College professors, looking confounded
All of God's scoldings were certainly founded
God was scolding, the verbiage was heated
He gave me pen and paper and said please be seated

You are not colleges, but institutions of hate
Piles of bowel waste you serve on a plate
Teaching garbage to young learners sent
Teaching protest, riot, revolt and dissent
I'm holding America who I love, in my hand
Your treasonous teachings cease and desist I demand

I am Almighty God, and you say I am not real
You'll change your mind when my wrath you'll soon feel

You're teaching genders in your mixed-up school
I said one gender stands, one sits on the stool
There are only two genders
I only created two

I have watched as America has grown to be great
For some reason you can't stand this and you're teaching hate
You want races to fight, and genders confused
You want our laws to be violated and abused
You are paid way too much for the garbage you serve
Now my plans are to give you everything you deserve

I do have a few colleges I protect with my hands
Shining examples of where higher learning stands
They've given me a place and they know I am real
They are not going to feel the pain you'll soon feel

The Peoples' Houses Need Repairs

Get the kids in congress some jellybeans
I see some of the little ones need a nap
I see a lot of temper tantrums
The speaker is sitting on socialism's lap

They string a lot of words together
Then they call their jabber a bill
They like to fight over who gets pork
While everyone else gets a bitter pill
Congress in their little school bubble
Finding buddies and chewing gum
Looks like they forgot how they got there
And even what country they come from

How did people ever get so stupid?
Weaponizing words and describing genders
They are supposed to be working for the American people
They are supposed to be constitution defenders
I think they should be renamed the playhouse
It's not the peoples house anymore
We need to find real adults to work for us
Throw the incompetent ones out the door

The senate is more like teenagers
Some are faithful defending their friends
Most are two-faced and can't be trusted
You really don't know where their loyalty ends

If you really know how to play the game
You'll own multiple properties, and your bank account grows
There are so many parties, with dining and gifts
A lot of them are crooks and everyone knows
The worst part is begging people for money
They plead for your money when it's time to vote
They like to add money to their growing coffers
But when we need something, they slit our throat

Socialism

The fall of humankind begins with a seed
A seed of disbelief and a hatred for God
Sown with infiltration into honest systems
Watered with a flood of lies
Cultivated by the greedy for more power
Watered again with the false promise of a better life
A better life to come and a better life for all
Goodness and love weeded out
Fertilized with equalness
And another soaking of division
Evil men plowing for the theft of freedom
A harvest of submission coming to fruition
The socialist reapers are waiting for the harvest
Man's fall stands leaning ripe for the harvest
Stop the reapers

Teachers Unions

The face in the window looked out one day
It saw a big file being carried all the way
To a giant toilet, the file was checked off the list
Then the toilet was flushed, no more to exist
Your teachers' unions have become vile
That's what I find as I check your file

You're money grubbers and children haters
You brainwash the young, you're America's traitors
Your mission isn't caring for hard working teachers
You've sold your unions to Marxist over reachers
A deceitful organization filled with greed
With corrupt politicians whose interests bleed

Where are the good books? Where is good learning?
Your common core books are only good for burning
Union coffers flooded with crooked money
Huge donations flow in like milk and honey
They are trying to change the next generation's soul
Oh, what fools, God is still in control
It's time to destroy the teachers union
It's time to get back to God's communion
God is going to take the teachers unions down
I watched them get flushed; in corruption they'll drown

The Different War

It was a different kind of war
A war for minds as games were played
The end was constantly delayed
You fought to keep your sanity
A painful mental war

It was a different kind of war
Pain was felt by us, the sane
Watching evil brought great pain
A war was waged to bring back truth
Incarcerated by the press

So goes war on a grander scale
With expert chess players making moves
Revealing those hiding Satan's hooves
When masks came off some gasped with fright
Though executions brought delight

Sanity is what we bled
As comms and Q drops filled our head
At times it all seemed so absurd
We retreated to God's word
There we dwelled till we felt well
We went back for more mental hell
Truth addiction was real, my friend
In wars you fight to the bitter
Or sweet end

The Right Time

I wondered why some eyes cannot see
You tell them the truth but for them it can't be
God said some have slumber to close their eyes
They're not ready to handle or see things wise
I've kept their eyes closed for their own protection
In my timing
I'll have them look my direction

Start Praying

The earth was brown
Something was missing
The falling rain
And the dry earth kissing
The earth was still
No trees were swaying
The voices were few
And none of them praying
God was gone
Now nothing will live
He's turned his back
There's no love to give
No love, no life
What's left was dwindling
No God, No love
What's left is kindling

It's Time

I heard the thunders boom and roar
They spoke of all man's grievous wars
They spoke God's awesome prophesies
Of what was yet to come
A warning to you mortal man
Get it together while you still can
Get it together before it's too late
Time is waning and God's opening the gate

The lightning struck and a question arose
Is man ready? And the thunder boomed "No!"
Many are coming, too many still slow
So many unbelievers, they surely won't go
They're slow to accept God, slow to forgive
I don't know how many of these will live

The lightning cracked and the thunder replied
There's no place to run and no place to hide
The judgement is coming, it's almost at hand
I don't know how many remaining will stand

Get it together mortal man
Get it together while you still can
Get it together before it's too late
The angels with trumpets are lining the gate

Lightning struck and the thunder broke silence
Woe to you who love sin and violence
Your garment is death and your destiny hell
If you think you are smarter than God, then farewell
Still, some are coming, they're changing their ways
The slow better hurry, there aren't many days
God who is awesome, his mercy is great
Gave us Jesus Christ our Lord, he's our key to the gate

Awesome thunder and I heard the voice
Say to everyone mortal "you must make your choice"

A warning to you mortal man
Get it together while you still can
Get it together before it's too late
They're calling the numbers to enter the gate

The Riots

The face was going to bed, it was late and quiet
A quick look out the window, what the hell? A dam riot!
The godless, selfish rioters were smashing peoples' dreams
Businesses, people built up were busted at the seams
Burning and looting and smashing the glass
Many paid and organized by an evil ruling class
Tearing cities down to gain a form of control
They used racism and hatred to promote their sick goal
The good people were helpless
Their dreams up in smoke
Only our Lord saw everything
Every rioter will choke
God has a video he's going to play
To each rioter, when it's their turn on judgement day
Funny thing is, not one of them will stand
Unless they repent, they will suffer God's hand

The face told God "I wish I was there with a gun"
I would have blown new holes in the asses of some
Or at least have something noiseless, perhaps a slingshot
I could pelt the rioters with coals burning hot
Only vengeance belongs to God, and it's worse
Those rioters will regret that they did not disperse

Our Leader

In the face of defeat stand tall
Hold your head high as truth prevails
The appearance of defeat can be deceit
As lies are flooded in waves and gales

Great leader with Almighty God's hand upon you
You walk through fires all day and all night
Although your enemies strive to harm you
You walk onward through the fires upright

Politics has become a vile hole
Where rats do nest and store their feces
Where lies are meant to be believed
The evilest of men do as they please

Stand tall, our chosen man of God
Keep taking them down with God's two-edged sword
Watch as God steadies the scales
He will strengthen you, leaving your enemies floored

Bring them down from their high places
Down so low they will welcome the hole
The masses have found you to be God's man
As evil is stripping our nation's soul

The light shines on you, great leader, our brother
God's light makes darkness go away
Shine the light, our beloved Trump of God
God's light will show us the way

Word Babies

Hurt feelings babies, still changing your own diapers
It's time for a change, your pull-ups stink
You are way too old to be nursing word pacifiers
It's time to grow up and have a stiff drink
We've been saying "he" and "she" since the beginning of time
Get over your tantrums to throw words away
Take your poopy fingers out of your pull-ups
Go put on some big pants and learn how to play

Word Ward

The face pulled the curtain back to look out into the yard
Instantly being transported to a hospital ward
Syringes of word anti-bodies, eye salves for erasing
For every new injustice the woke ones were chasing

Susan is in the hospital
Someone used the word "she"
It's going to take a week to heal
Good thing someone didn't say "he"

Gordon is in the hospital too
Someone said the name Fort Bragg
Those words have caused him so much pain
Gordon is hurting, and that's a real drag

When you see Susan, just use the term "the person"
Please don't use the terms "he" and "she"
A serious operation may be pending
Susan may need major brain surgery

The next time any of you see Gordon
Don't say Jefferson, Washington or Lincoln
Those names are truly so painful and offensive
If Gordon even hears them his mind will be gone

The nurses on the word ward are falling apart
They don't know what words to say, flatulence or fart
They aren't allowed to say white rice or brown
They don't know if their patients want a doctor or a clown

Eric in room seven still needs his burping
Check Barry's sippy cup, he's not sipping he's slurping
Dr. Smart went looking for the biggest needle he could find
The next person who corrects him is getting jabbed in their behind

We still need to make our rounds
In our eyesight ward twenty-two
Reginald over there can barely live
After viewing President Lincoln's statue

We have Adam and Omar screaming in pain
They say they would rather die
Than to ever view our history's statues again

But first we will check on Hilary
Everything she looks at she sees racism and hate
Tomorrow the surgeon will remove her eyes
I hope he's on time and not late

The nurses have had it, and wonder if they should retire
Or
Maybe it would just be better to set both wards on fire

Throw Down

He fell from grace
The vile one chained
Behind the throne
Of God's ordained
The wrath of him
Who sits on the throne
Will soon unchain Satan
Out he'll be thrown
Heaven will clamor
Mighty voices rejoicing
The devil's been cast down
Heaven joyfully voicing
But woe to the earth
For the devil has come
Woe to the earth
For the devil is handsome

The Cat and the Bird

There was a cat that caught a bird
Sharp claws caught and brought the bird down
Then the cat inflicted torture
Pouncing on the bird it had on the ground
The cat let the bird try to fly
Just to take it down once more
While playing the game, the bird got away
The bird had won this unfair war

Now we will call corruption the cat
We will say freedom is the bird
The corrupt cat was slinking and prowling about
The bird freedom was singing as corruption purred
Corruption tried to kill the freedom
Torturing freedom with lockdowns and laws
But freedom was still strong and escaped to be free
As corruption was taken down by another with big claws

Here kitty kitty, what do you have to say?
The bird flipped you off as it flew away
Corruption has power but freedom has wings
When it comes to the take down
It depends on who sings

The Machine

The face looked out the window and said "what does that mean?
On the patio was some sort of vending machine
The light was blinking the words "make a selection"
It pushed itself and said "you won a stolen election"

Next there was a yard sign advertising actor for rent
With a picture of America's fake president
There were people with little, tiny eyes, they were unaware
They didn't notice votes were stolen, they just didn't care
With those little, tiny eyes, they just could not see
Their eyes were for fake news they watched on tv

The shame of it all is they're all going to fall
When the shit show comes to an end
The good people's machine is going to clean
The dirty system and the election they'll mend

I don't think the actor will get any work
He is just controlled, and he's kind of a jerk
The crooked election workers, they're going to pay
They'll be going to jail, they won't have a say

The righteous winner is going to stand once more
With a joyous celebration, his supporters will roar
We will thank God Almighty for helping us fight
Stolen elections are wrong, God's people made it right

The Thorn

A great man endured so much scorn
To the evil ones he was a thorn
They always tried to take him out
But the thorn went deeper on its route
The evil ones were digging deeper
They tried to kill the people's keeper
They dug a hole so deep they bled
Writhing in pain, the thorn went to the head
The evil blood spilled its disorder
The blood spilled on their new world order
Their blood poured greed and lies were born
To hide their child rape, murder and porn
The thorn was really doing its job
It caused the wound to open and throb
God's truth inflicted, will bring a great loss
To the evil who scorned God and reviled the cross
Plans to remove God will never succeed
God has an army of thorns for this need
Through time God created great men to be born
Sometimes he chooses one to be his thorn

Political What?

Don't lay your political correctness on me
The weight of your burden, I cannot bear
Sparing your feelings from everyday talk
Grow up because I don't care
Did you ever hear of the sticks and the stones?
Did you hear that they could break your bones?
If you want to be a big kid now
These words should ring true
Words are just words....
(They can't hurt you)

Other Faces

The face looked out the window to see
Many other faces just like me
Everyone looking around and around
Every face looking for truth to be found
We are living in trying times my friend
Some felt the world was going to end
Forces trying to control with power
Some new misery every hour
Lies just fell like falling rain
Rules to grieve us and cause us pain
We looked at each other and all did nod
It was us, we still had a mighty God
Though at times we thought it grim
At times our hope had whittled slim
Our lights at times a little dim
We still had God, we still had him
He always had the mightiest power
It is his timing, he'll choose the hour
Then he will let his fury fly
By his side, we will stand by
He will give us power to stand
We'll fight to fix the troubled land
To clean up politics as well

While he threatens them with hell
God Almighty will clean the earth
He'll give his chosen newfound worth
All the windows with watching faces
Now waiting for God to give them their places
Some windows showed that the faces were gone
As we each got our orders, we had to move on

Real Justice

Swift justice
God demands
Evil languishing
Has no pros
Expedite evil
To God's throne
To God
Not to death rows

Truthful Troops

March on soldier of truthfulness
With a singing cadence geared to the right
Right, right, right left right
Marching through a confused land
Marching with scepters of truth in their hand

Fight those troops, fight the wayward squads
The squads who parade their vicious mouths
With gnashing teeth and serpent tongues
They submerge the masses in lies
With huge lips, they even try the wise

Soldiers carry your truth preservers
Throw them to the drowning with outstretched arms
Rescue them from the flood of lies
Help them to the strong land
Far away from the sinking sand

March on soldiers of truthfulness
Sturdy the bars for incarcerating
Capture the squads with grotesque large mouths
With mouths too large for their faces
Confine them in your truthful bars and braces

March on soldiers and fight the fight
Fight the underground squads of evil
Concealed billionaires with money to burn
Reveal them and pile their money for a bonfire
Watch it burn wearing your truthful attire

They squander their money to buy more power
Building a deceitful house of cards
The marching troops cause the land to tremble
Their cards cannot stand, unstable, they fall
Offspring of Satan, they try to deceive all

March on troops with that singing cadence
The giant mouthed evil doers are contained
They can tell each other their lies while detained
After so many lies, they will want the truth
After so many lies, even they do
They will want to stew on the truth

The Wrath was Subsiding

The face opened the window to let in fresh air
The visions were slowing, there were fewer to share
There was a lot going on, if you could see
A lot of wrongs to write, were given to me
The wrath was subsiding though it was still there
When the grievances came, my ink gave them flare
My heart, my mind, my pen and soul
All belonged to God. His will, my goal
As the messages slowed
I felt a twinge of rejection
A note stuck on the window said
Go write your own section
Anything you want
It will be your selection
I took my writing in another direction
The note said P.S.
I may have something to add
The face looked up to God and spoke
Thank you, Lord, I'm glad

Snow From Heaven

It was snow from heaven
It was no ordinary snow
It was weighty and fell straight down
Showers of lace, falling from the sky
It fell as if it were the breath of God
As if it had a purpose to speak
To say to humankind, slow down
To reflect on this hampering beauty
Although it was falling, it had a stillness
Be still and know that I am, God's word said
If you had a good heart, you could feel peace deep inside
If you had a good soul, you could feel solace deep inside
If you belonged to God, you could feel his presence
If you were evil, you cussed it
God was calling and you didn't answer
I was standing beneath the angels' gowns
It was snow sent from heaven

King of Kings

Rolling hills of faithful women and men
For miles they came to see their King
For a crown and a blessing, amen, amen
So be it, their faithful song they sing
Blessed be our King, they sing in their song
Their King victorious, gloriously lives
They praise and worship their Lord ever long
As eternal life and salvation he gives
Blessed be our Lord, blessed be our King
He is the living word of almighty God they sing
He paid the ransom for our lives we now bring
Rolling hills of the faithful's love they bring

When I Leave

With no tear in my eye
I will not tell this world good-bye
This world has been no friend of mine
I'll return to where I see love shine
My Lord has promised long ago
He will show me home, when I must go
No memory of me will remain
For friends I barely made a gain
Family only caused a stain
Though I tried, it was in vain
This world will not follow me
My Lord is all I want to see
I will not leave anyone behind
For I had no one, all my love is thine
Though Lord these two found no disdain
For I so loved the birds and rain

Lily

Lily, you were a four-foot giant
Not very tall but towering in spirit
I lovingly remember you
The love you showed me
The kind words you always spoke to me
The praying I watched you do
I was always welcome in your house
You often offered me a stick of gum
When I was little, you were big
Now that I'm big, you were huge

Rain? What Rain?

Oh Lord, the rain has disappeared
Long gone, and nowhere to be found
The flowers tire and leaves start falling
Cracks wide open on brown ground
Lord it's dry, six feet down
Like gaping wounds, the ground now wears
It's just too much for righteous men
Forgive them for their swears

Rage

Explosive rage will spew its matter
Rage can discharge with a force
Like broken pipes that gush and flood
But broken pipes feel no remorse

Remorse

Remorse can be a grievous burden
The eyes of God a glaring stare
Gravity from the hand of God
Can make this burden hard to bear

Forgiveness

Forgiveness is a saving vessel
It offers rescue to your soul
If you climb in, it can take you to
A place where you'll be whole

Broken Heart

She was so sad
Her heart was broken
Her husband died
No more love you's spoken
With children to raise
All on her own
She never remarried
She stayed alone
Her love for her husband
Unfathomably deep
No love could replace him
She often would weep
Broken hearts
Are different for all
Some hearts can add love
Some answer the call
Some hearts stay sad
They live with the pain
She waits for the time
When she'll see him again
Some loves are eternal
They never end
Some hearts stay broken
They never mend

God's Man

The wilderness made him
He was made for the wilderness
The rugged beauty made him rugged
He hunted game, and caught fish with finesse

He was a great wilderness builder
Created by necessity and outstanding math skills
He could build anything anywhere
Near shores or out in the untamed hills

The wilderness was the art he admired
If you think he didn't notice, you would be wrong
The music he heard and admired the most
Was any wild bird singing its song

He had a wild perseverance
A born in desire to see anything through
He couldn't give up and he didn't give in
Though, he just changed a strategy or two

He wasn't lonely, he had a woman
There was no hen-pecking, she catered to him
Mutual admiration and love for the wild
He would pull her close, when he had a whim

Strength in his body and tender in his heart
He would look you in the eye to measure your soul
His was stamped God's, and he lived in the wild
He was God's man and he lived up to the roll

New Party

I used to belong to the donkey party
They changed their ways, so I had to move on
Then I joined the elephant party
They lost my confidence and now I'm gone

It's time for a new American party

Everyone with morals is now invited
We want a party that is united
We want the constitution followed as cited
We want crooked politicians indicted

The animal parties are really just one
They've sold themselves out to everyone
They beg for your vote and beg for your money
When you want their help, they laugh, like it's funny

We want a party that stands for the people
A party for America, God and the steeple
We want a party with no race or gender baiters
We want a party who punishes traitors

Everyone's invited if you feel the same
All we need now is a very cool name

Shine The Light

When darkness falls, beware, beware
You don't know what will fall from hidden air
It may be something you don't want to see
It needs to happen to set the truth free
It needs to happen, so let it be
Let the light see every corner of the unfolding
Shine the light in the dark, show what evil's been holding
Then keep the light on for those who feel fear
Let the light shine and keep the light near

Be Proud

If the Lord God made you brown
Then be proud to be brown

If the Lord God made you black
Then be proud to be black

If the Lord God made you tan
Then be proud to be tan

If the Lord God made you white
Then be proud to be white

It was the Lord God who created the races
He chose our skin colors our hair and our faces

No shaming allowed for who people are
No shaming allowed for the color of their skin
No shaming allowed for the choice wasn't ours
Look in the mirror and look within
And be proud

And God saw everything He had made
And behold it was very good

Genesis 1:31

Pray for Rain

I felt the quaking aspens quake
They were watching the weeping willows weep
They saw the evergreens were turning brown
There was no more rain falling down

The purple smoke trees went up in smoke
The burning bushes long dried, have died
And rarely could you find but a cluster of leaves
For all the poor little birds to hide

God was sending a message loud and clear
Start praying now, start praying here
If you would just humble yourselves and pray
I will cause the rain to come your way

If you would seek my face and reach for my hand
If you would turn and leave your wicked ways behind
I'll send rain from heaven to fall on your land
I will heal your land and save humankind

God doesn't make a promise he doesn't keep
It's sad to watch a dry weeping willow weep

The Inheritance

Greed thicker than blood doth kill
In kin it strikes an evil chord
Want for money, derides ties
As siblings lie in family gore
Executor with a lust for lucre
Monetary gains outweigh
Dividing remnants of a life
That's long since passed away
Let the greedy thief betray
The wishes bestowed in a will
She doled out a meager pittance
Her kin betrayed for a dollar bill
The lawyer evil in his share
Who did not suffer family pain
Siphoned more blood from her kin
He corrupted his self a heathy gain
The vilest of stings can a sibling bring
And we will be kin no more

No Regrets

What is there to regret
Don't trouble yourself with these feelings
Let bygones be bygones
Leave sleeping dogs lay
Don't beat a dead horse
Don't dwell on your sorrows
Yesterdays are gone
Be happy today
We still have abundant tomorrows

Could, Should, Would Have

If I could go back in time
I would have made better choices
I would not make the same mistakes
Or listen to the wrong voices

I could have kept to myself more
Keeping my voice more quiet
I could have done things differently
Eating a better diet

I would not have repeated rumors
But that's what people do
I could have stayed at some jobs longer
But I had to try something new

I could have done more for my mom
Now that I'm looking back
I could have had more confidence
That's one thing I did lack

I would have kept myself more pure
But circumstances prevailed
I would not have dated a criminal
Who kept getting himself jailed

What I should have done is pursue an art
Though I played guitar and failed
I should not have sent a couple of letters
But it was too late, they were mailed

I could have done so much better
Now that I'm wiser I see
But if I would have chosen other paths
Then I would not be me

Special Place

It was real, just unknown
Clear water babbled in the brook
The sun glowed red between the branches
No one was there to look
It was a haven, heavenly
Singing songbirds filled the air
A few large rocks where one could rest
Lovely, though no one was there

A fragrant breeze now stirred still air
The smell of bee balm carried through
Could this place be here on earth?
It's there, though no one knew
This is where God's spirit passes
Unknown to man, God is aware
When He finds dear souls, he loves
He will bring them there

Fall Leaves

Leaves of yellow and red
Orange and brown
They curl and twirl
They float to the ground
In a windy ride they're blown
"Hey", not so rough and not so far from where they've grown
When they fall, they want to stay close to home

Glorious Hill

We lived on top of the hill
That hill, that hill, that glorious hill
When it snowed it was the place to be
We froze our feet and the spills and the thrills
On that hill we were carefree
That panel truck hood and some saucers and sleds
And the neighborhood kids that slipped and slid
The breath and the laughter
And the dry socks after
We lived, that's what we did
How many kids could you fit on a hood
Five or six and we still slid good
And trudging up the hill wasn't thought of as a chore
We went up the hill so we could go down more
That hill, that hill
What a glorious hill
To us kids that were poor, we were rich and still
I can still hear the laughter
Of the slipping and the sliding
Of the neighbor kids on that hill

More Birds Please

Give me today my daily birds
And may I have an extra share?
If so, may I have even more?
More flying birds
And eating birds
And drinking birds
And bathing birds
Could I please have more nesters too?
I watch them gather twigs and strings
Dry leaves and twine, fine nesting things
A shred of plastic, feathers and hair
And don't forget the mud
And fill my trees with singing birds
Chirpers and tweeters welcome too
Winter, spring, summer and fall
I need more than a few

Color Me Summer

Gravel roads and wheat straw baled
Two young hawks learning to fly
How beautiful the land is veiled
With wildflowers, grass and grains grown high
How lovely are the full leaved trees
Adorned with green and summer hues
When gently swaying in the breeze
The decorate the rural views
How welcome are the summer rains
That give drink to the toiled fields
And grow the heads on stalks of grains
And give abundance to the yields
Beholding all of summer's show
I can barely comprehend
All this splendor soon must go
As autumn ushers in the end

Good Night Lord

It's late and I can't go to bed
I can't seem to part with God
I stay up late to be with him
Until I start to nod
God said he would never
Leave or forsake me
So, I'm trying to return the favor
I stay up late to be with him
But I'm always the first to waiver

Not So Bad Afterall

When your troubles seem insurmountable
You wonder how much more your plate can hold
After everything else, what else can go wrong?
You feel left out in the cold

You see mountains on the horizon
Mountainous burdens, you feel they are so high
Those mountains surely must be hiding canyons
You wonder how you will ever get by

Remember when Jesus walked through a wall
"Be thou removed" to the mountains, he said
He raised the dead and gave sight to the blind
With five loaves and a couple fish, the multitudes were fed

No mountains are too high when you call his name
You may find a couple passages will be a little tight
He was walking beside you, when you were alone
The mountains will turn out to be clouds, in the light

The Fight

Like the stars in the night, are the righteous
Fighting for justice in a dark world
Speaking out
To subdue the bitter wind of lies
Trodding through the crusted snow
They do not become weary
They trudge through carrying the banner of victory
The standard of freedom
Given to humankind from the Almighty
They are leaving behind the defeated
The conquered soldiers of socialism
They were a once upon a time remnant army
From other countries and times
This time they were destroyed
And are no more
The flag of freedom flies high
The freedom fighters victorious
With their blood, sweat and tears they will do it again
They are the army empowered by God
The enemy was destroyed
And is no more

Gifts

Grace and mercy came to me
They clothed me in their glorious wear
They covered me, my shame, my sins
Mine were more than I could bear
Though undeserved they gave to me
The gifts not earned or bought for cost
They follow Him who seeks and saves
They are the gifts he gives the lost

Church in the Garden

Here in the flower garden
The wind chimes are my church bells
The blue sky is my cathedral ceiling
The rocks are a reminder of life's hardships
Once a burden to move
Now a reminder of strength
I can look upon them with satisfaction
Yet a small measure of sadness and regret
The flowers around them decorate long ago pain
The painted metal flowers cannot die
Though sometimes they need a new coat of paint
Like all of us who repent, and we are new again
The spirit of God is welcome here
So would be God himself
He might say "you have some weeds still"
"I can forgive them"
"I'll help you water"
(Thunder)

Do You See What I See

See the berries withering
And the flowers fading bloom

See the dark skies now encroaching
Whispering impending doom
Do you see or do you sleep
While you are wide awake
Living dead, for heaven's sake
See the devil and his rake
You don't care for other people
You see that's a big mistake

If your heart would thaw
Your eyes would see a new world calling
You could give back what you took
You could see the error of your ways
And have another look

See the berries on the trees
And the flowers in full bloom

Setting Sun

He just worked and lived
No one ever gave him a helping hand
No one ever helped him along the way
He wasn't born with any silver spoons
He never heard God's word until today

He never found love
He was open but it never came
Never did a woman ever look his way
He long ago gave up on a family
Everyday life seemed just more of the same

He perceived life unfair
Working so hard and still just getting by
He didn't get the promotion he earned
With a chip on his shoulder from an unfair lie
It was just another page of unfairness turned

Once a wayward son
Now the sun is setting on his day
On a lifetime of just not getting it right
He has found his way today

Once a wayward son
Now a son of God today
His memories of an empty life without love
Have now all gone away

One sun sets as another son rises
One breath ceases as another wind blows
Some tears well up as the rain falls down
He deemed his life dull, but God says it glows

He thought he was not loved but now he knows
He's crossed over, there he goes

I Rode the Wind

I rode the wind for many years
I dropped some seeds throughout the land
I watered some with heartfelt tears
I wasted some on rocks and sand
I skimmed the waters, stopped in fogs
I fell flat in the muck and mire
But I'd crawl out of the muddy bogs
To fly with eagles, sometimes higher
I had no reins to steer a course
No map or compass to compel
I gave my life unto the force
With the keys and power over hell
When hell reached to take my breath
God reached out to do the same
Triumphant power over death
To anyone called by his name
No wind, I settled on the earth
Upon a path where few would go
Stones paved salvation, love and worth
There, I found more seeds to sow

Did You Know Her

They spoke of her harshly, they treated her cruel
They pointed their fingers when she went to school
When she was older, they gave her no rest
They wouldn't accept her though she tried her best

She was so forgiving, no grudges she'd hold
She tried to make friends, but they all were so cold
She sighed as she wondered
What brought this about?
Was it just being poor that was keeping her out?
She looked at her clothes, they had always been used
She's just dirty poor trash, they laughed, and they mused

Her face displayed beauty and grace filled her walk
Though she was not worldly
That made people talk
She said things like...God bless you...Jesus is Lord
When they gathered, they'd recall her words
And they roared
Though friendless, she walked with the Lord by her side
They treated her harshly and so sadly, she died
Happy to give
Sad to live
Life had dealt a cruel blow
Happy to die
Too sad to cry
Her love was held so low

Humble Kingdom

A man's farm is a woman's kingdom
Behold her gardens and her trees
She's planned and planted all her subjects
Many on her hands and knees
Fruit trees, nut trees, berries, flowers
Vegetables and herbs she grows
Giving freely of the excess
The Lord has blessed her, and it shows
She mows and hoes
And sows and grows
And shows her love and knows it flows
She seeds and weeds
And feeds some's needs
And bleeds good deeds and then she glows
She lives to give
And gives to live
And nary has she any woes
She's queen, and crowned with humble measure
A man's farm, and her kingdom grows
It's God's farm and her kingdom grows

Native Soul

She sits in peace
She strings the beads without a care
Her mind is free
You'll find no place for evil there
Her heart is full of love and ways
The ways her people lived life for
Her baskets are stacked
Her beadwork packed
She'll sell them at the tribe's gift shop
Her wares are quality, they'll be on top
They'll go to homes
Where thankful people bless her hands
She's talented
She'll make more wares to fill demands
A candle burns
Dusk is calling for the night
She says her prayers
She thanks the great one for his might
She thanks him for his love and grace
Her glory soars on eagle's wings
She dreams she'll see him face to face
Then wakes up to the beads she strings

The Gang

Kevin came in our yard
He started to beat up brother Ron
All the little kids started screaming
Then they all piled on
They were brutally pinching Kevin
They were viciously clawing his skin
They beat his head as hard as they could
With a hard plastic bowling pin
That'll teach you to beat up brother Ron
They thought poor Ron was dying
Then Kevin stopped and he got up
He left the yard, and he was crying
Kevin was a big scary kid
But he was whipped by the gang
Kevin, you stay off our yard
Or your head will get another bang

Another War

The art of war
A sneaky thrill
Strategies and coded names
Covert moves
A strike, a slay
War games
Exposing foes
A blissful art
Brazen plots to execute
Captured dregs of society
Orange jumpsuits aren't they cute
Take downs
Liars slaughtered
With two-edged swords
Evil shown and truth restored
Distinguished men with skillful tactics
Cleaning up our dirty politics
War heroes

When Troubles Come

When troubles come, now the redwoods call
To search the heart as deep as the trees are tall
With new perspective, worries will not show
Strong like trees, we won't let troubles grow
While giant trees can dwarf us in their space
The awe we feel takes worries from our face
Nothing good can be added or gained
When troubles or worries are entertained
Now as we pause and consider the trees
We see troubles are small
Compared to the grandeur of these

Sifted Snow

I walk in soft and sifted snow
So pure white, it has a glow
With glitter sprinkled for a show
In blissful solitude I go
Snow so pure can soothe a soul
When weariness has had control
The sky dark gray with pure snow falling
I almost hear the angels calling
So beautiful, my eyes could cry
Though tears might freeze, so I'll just sigh

Remember the Daisies

She gathered daisies and quite a lot
She sat and plucked the petals out
He loves me and he loves me not
Her ritual and she devout

Plucking, pulling, chant repeating
Persisting till the petals gone
She realized this was defeating
He loves me nots were all that won

Staring where her flowers lay
Wishing they were in a vase
She got up to pick some more
That's when she saw his face

He was tending to the flowers
He was looking over her way
She came near to pick more daisies
He spoke and said "please stay"

Can you sit with me on the garden seat?
Can you keep me company for a while?
He handed her a bouquet of daisies
She returned a glowing smile
She pulled just one out of the bunch
She plucked the petals, one by one
He loves me and he loves me not
This time, he loves me won

Time soon brought their wedding day
Daisies overflowing everywhere
In the garden where she met her man
She wore daisies in her hair

Long Live My Heart

Heart, you pound and heart, you throb
I'm sorry you're stressed
I hate my job
I hate the smell
I hate the place
I hate my boss
He hates my face
(My ass as well)
I don't feel well
Someday I'll tell him
No! Today I'll tell him
Good-bye! Farewell!
Adios tough guy
You go to hell
Get another work horse, buddy
Get another whipping post
I'll get out the champagne
I'll make my own toast
To my heart, to my health
To my new mental wealth
To new skies and new grass
To my boss
I have class

Beautiful Day

It's a beautiful day in our neighborhood
That bully Dave moved out last night
We won't be getting bullied today
He won't be provoking us to fight

Seems the sky looks brighter today
We've lived in fear for the last three years
I saw the movers arrive all dressed in black
They packed Dave up, then sat and drank beers
I watched the movers work so fast and hard
They had a big roll of carpet, it really looked heavy
They were all done way before dawn
The yard's cleaned out, even that old chevy

Last night was a beautiful night
The moon and stars were brighter than ever
The neighbors came out to wave good-bye
Bully Dave is gone (forever)

That moving truck looked like Marvin's down the street
The tow truck I saw, looked like Jake's
But it was so dark out, I could barely see
I think Dave moved to the Great Lakes

A police officer drove by and said "looking good"
It's a beautiful day in our beautiful neighborhood

Spirit Run

The sky was gray, and the lightning struck white
Uneasy horses ran all night
They raced the wind with tails high
Only they know the reason why
Run horses run to your delight
Run till you get your spirits right
Run like lightning until you're done
Who knows, maybe you are having fun

Sometimes people will run away
When lightning strikes their skies of gray
Some feel the winds of changing come
And so, they run, not all but some

Run horses run to your delight
Run until the dark is light
You must run and I must sleep
We both have journeys we must keep

Thought For the Road

Now your years are old, and your days are spent
You're reflecting on how they came and went
You sit with gray or thinning hair
Just last week, you were forty, you'll swear
You sit and think about past years
You've maybe cried your share of tears
You shared your life with family and friends
Some surely pushed you, to your wits ends
You remember giving help and hope
When someone was tangled in life's rope
You know you shared some good advice
With people, some bad, and some were nice
Did you do your work as to the Lord?
To help you reach your end reward
At times you gave forgiveness or love
To someone in need when push came to shove
Did you believe in Jesus Christ our king
This is more important than anything
If for some reason, you're feeling uncertain
Listen my dear, it's never too late
Just pray to God and ask for His mercy
He's waiting for you so don't wait

The Living Farm

It's here I find peace, on the farm where I live
With the trees I have planted, and the fruit that they give
In the gardens where vegetables thrive and produce
There are bountiful berries, I have for my use
Dear Lord, the colors of flowers that grow
Some colors don't even have names that I know
Here birds entertain me and brighten my days
I love all their movements and their funny ways
Though I like the sun, it's the overcast days
When rest joins my peace, and the calmness that stays
Rain falls and waters the life that I've sown
It's here, I feel the love that you've shown
Lord, fall is coming, as summer is going
New colors exalting the season now showing
The seasons of labor will come to an end
Starry eyed, I'll watch the snowfall you send
Then winter will sleep under blankets of snow
I'll be quite tired and be somewhat slow
You're Lord of the seasons, they come, and they go
Lord, every four seasons, I'm older
I know

Life at Work

I feel I'm riding a merry-go-round pony
Trying to grab the ring
I just thought if I could grab it
A real nice prize it would bring
Then it would be over
No more spinning around
But my pony's too small
Too far away
And too close to the ground

Now work turned into bumper cars
I tried to do some bumping
Only I'm the one who everyone bumps
I've taken quite a thumping

There's no way to get ahead
On a wheel with so many seats
Round and round and up and down
On a wheel that no one beats

I don't want to be just a cog
That works to turn the wheel
I want to be the key that turns it on
That's exactly how I feel
(Or maybe I could be the wheel)

She Unloved

So sad a story to partake
For she unloved the earth did quake
It trembled sadness, tremored sorrow
It quaked as though there'd be no morrow
She sat lonely, sadly keeping
She alone, while love lie sleeping

For she unloved the earth did quake
Stirring to let love awake
It summoned love to come to her
To soothe her like the richest myrrh
To fill her heart till lonely flees
It found a man down on his knees

From long lain slumber love awoke
It found its way in glorious stride
For love awakes in its own time
It nurtures places to abide
And she now loved, her sadness eased
The earth did rest, for it was pleased

Little Girl

He looks like a decent guy
But he's a predator inside
He's been dating another new woman
With a little girl by her side
Her demeanor has changed
She says "momma, he's hurting me"
Kids will say the strangest things
Her momma is in love and couldn't see

He's abusing the girl
She's grasping for help with her words
No one understands or listens to her
And her words fly away like birds
How much more can she bear
He's a vile monster inside
Now he's gone too far abusing her
And the little girl almost died

Another victim of child abuse
Sweet little girl's words fell like lead
All those she reached out to were ashamed
They didn't hear what the little girl said

Glistening Gold

He left his wife and his children
For a greater love at the bar
For the cold glistening gold liquid
Till the thoughts of his family were far

He went to work every morning
After work he didn't go home
He longed to hold his gold liquid
With other women he would roam

His family only grew poorer
Their love for him turned to hate
He gave up his role as family
He kept drinking and coming home late

When he wasn't drunk, he was mean
He couldn't wait to go drink
When he left, his children were happy he fled
Good riddance dad, you stink

His wife always stayed beside him
But loneliness took its toll
He gave his family a bad name
His family had no soul

His children now grown, some troubled
Most of them hated each other
Thanks to their dad for being a drunk
And for ruining their mother

Thank you, parents, for giving them life
That's all they have to thank you for
A houseful of strangers they grew to be
Rich in bar life, but family poor

Patience for the Plan

The face looked out and saw good things too
God was always with us, helping good people through
There were even times he would cause us to laugh
When he smacked down the wicked with his mighty staff
The government dictates, political muck and mire
God's hands protected us, when we traveled higher
We had to learn patience, see, he had a plan
God's word foretold us, what he wanted from man
Patience was hard, it was grueling to some
Though we had to practice it, to see more souls come
God is calling, what a beautiful sound
It's heard by those who were lost, but now found
When found, they start looking out windows, like me
They are God's chosen, when they have eyes that see

The Jewelry Box

She opened her jewelry box
It held her jewels
Her jewels weren't jewelry
But a pair of black shoes
Open back slip-ons
They had a flat heel
One sole was cracked
But they had a special feel

She wore those shoes
Every day since he died
She had to wear them
If she didn't, she cried
Those were the shoes
She had on that day
The day he gave them to her
Was the day he passed away

She wore those shoes
Every day all day long
They helped her remember
He wanted her to be strong

She lost him to cancer
He left her that day
His gift was a memory
She wore every day

She walked for miles in his shoes
She walked for miles wearing the blues
She walked for miles, those shoes paid their dues
She walked for miles in his shoes

Time has passed and she's wearing new shoes
His pair she treasures and treats them like jewels
Some soles wear out and some souls move on
The memories of loved souls will never be gone

Lover, Lover

Lingering by the window well
Gazing at the sky turned gray
Pondering this question deep
Will a lover come my way?
Lover, lover where are you?
Somewhere in another day
Somewhere in the night like me
I'm waiting here for you my love
I'm waiting an eternity
Lover, I did search for you
I waited sad and tarried long
It seems it should not be my fate
That I would ever hear love's song
Lover, lover, our paths lost
As destiny cries not to be
I'm numbered in with vanished hopes
Sorrowful I, will not be, we

The Harvest

Bring the bless-ed harvest in
For it is surely ripe to pick
Though some stalks were sparsely filled
Other stalks were full and thick
The harvester will reap the fields
When there he finds enough for sheaves
He will thrash and separate
Believers from the tares and thieves

Bad Boy Mike

Mike you were a bad, bad boy
You tied little Patty to your front yard tree
You had circus peanuts that you would not share
You tied her so tight; she couldn't get free
You hurt little Patty and you did not care
Mike you were a bad, bad boy
You need a good spank with your pants pulled down
And to be quite frank
Your parents didn't raise you very well

Mike you were a cruel, cruel boy
You were vicious when you called her names
What's wrong with you treating little girls this way
Your mom and dad sure aren't raising you very well
I sure hope someone thumps your gourd someday

Mike you were a mean, mean boy
You threw a rock-hard snowball and hit her in the eye
You deliberately squeezed it till it turned to ice
She screamed "my eye! My eye! And you made her cry
Mike you were never, never, ever, ever nice

Mike you were a bad, bad boy
You need a hard spank with your pants pulled down
And to be quite frank
Your parents didn't raise you very well

She's Gone

The flowers, though some blooming
They are overgrown and weedy
It seems no one wants to care for them
They just grow there looking needy
She's gone
The berries they need picking
There are apples hanging on the trees
No one wants to pick them
They are stopped by all the memories
She's gone
Now the bird feeders sit empty
And the birdbaths need some tending to
Birds come look and nothing is there
Though God feeds them
She always cared
She's gone
She's gone and she's not coming back
She's gone
There's a special kind of sadness
A more special kind of gladness
That she lived but she's not here with us
She's gone

Seasoning the Trees

The leaves were green a month ago
Summers wind made them blow
They were strong and they held fast
For as long as the wind would last

The leaves were gold a week ago
They were tired and they let go
Now the branches wearing twigs
Bare, they miss their autumn wigs

The snow came down a day ago
Snow filled branches wear a glow
Now the trees are winter dressed
With snow is when they like to rest

Today I'll walk amid the trees
I'll spend time with the Lord and these
Remembering how the seasons passed
Seasons and lives do not last

Tonight, Lord when I pray to you
I'll thank you for the trees you grew
The ones in heaven must be great
I long to see them Lord
But I can wait

Skip

Skip was born to serve

He was a dog just born to work
He had a purpose built into his soul
He wanted to be man's best friend
He didn't need teaching, he knew his role

He helped with the roundups
He ran off the pests
He barked at strangers he didn't trust
His tail would be wagging whenever he saw Joe
Protecting his farm to him was a must

He loved to go with Joe
He loved to go fishing with Joe at the lake
He was so excited when they caught a fish
He always got his share in his dish
They didn't mind taking a nap when they could
Joe didn't know a dog that was ever that good

He liked to go fishing, he liked to hunt
With the window rolled down Skip would bark at the air
Joe would talk and Skip seemed to listen
Joe loved to take Skip with him everywhere

One day Skip was not there
He didn't run up with his tail wagging
He wasn't anywhere Joe could see
Down by the water Skip took his last nap
Joe picked him up tenderly

Joe had to bury his partner that day
He kneeled and bowed his head to pray
As a good-bye tear slid down his face
This is what he had to say
Skip, you were a real good dog
God gave you to me, now he took you home
You'll have so many more places to roam
You're done working here, and now you're free
Skip, you were more than a dog to me

Giving Thanks

The face in the window looks out to see
A cardinal sitting in the tree
The bird sits and fluffs
It's feathers it puffs
It sits for a long while
It makes the face smile
The mouth on the face
Gives thanks for the bird
Aso thanking God almighty for his word
And for the special messages the window looking brings
The mouth on the face said "Lord, why me?"
God's spirit said it's because you can see
When you look out the window, you always look for me

Red Love

Red cardinal in a white birch tree
You are a fine divine sight to see
God has dressed you beautifully
Black mask and red feathers for me to see
When you stop and visit my tree
I wish that's where you'd always be
Red feather love is what I see
No charge for the bird food
The seed is free

Pure Snow

The snow falls
Calmness calls
Purity is falling
Outside of my walls
Snow is a blessing
As it is now dressing
The earth
For an angelic winter scene

The Table

Lay your weapons down, lay them down
Come and let us join together
At the table of common good
Let us first bless this table for God Almighty
He alone is the God of all
Here for all, is a plate of good will
Let us all have a heaping of humility
And serve us all, each one, a slice of forbearing
For we are all weary from war
Please pass the forgiveness and a heaving portion take all
For we are all famished from war
The flavor of forgiveness will be satisfying
Reach across the table and share with one another
Season your meals with truthfulness
Slice the grievance from your meat and set it aside

Your goblets have been filled with the water of life
Drink until your thirst is quenched
Drink until you have had your fill of war
The masses will eat the portions that are left
They are starving for peace
With outreached arms they are begging for their share
For a serving of peace in their bowls

Let us end this meal with a prayer to live
To live and let live
To give and forgive
To war no more
To stop the greedy warmongers who hunger for power
And thirst for blood
The deceitful warmongers with disregard for the lives of men
They demand more blood, and laugh
Let us leave this table of common good
Let us walk out satiated and only return as friends
The greedy warmongers can eat the crumbs and live
They can clean up the mess

My Love

If I could sing of my love for God
I would be singing forever
Or if I spoke of my love for my Lord
I would not stop speaking ever
If I could fill my thoughts with my Lord
I would never stop thinking
If I could not sing, talk or think of him
I would probably start drinking

Snow Flowers

Delicate flowers formed of snow
Exquisite, for eyes to behold
She carries them, her snow bouquet
She sees herself, if truth be told

The hands that planted summer's flowers
Ache with pain in stiffened joints
Fresh snow fell on winter's flowers
On remaining petals and points

She was once a summer flower
Now she's faded and the birds she feeds
Like flowers, she will rest through winter
Like faded flowers, she has few needs

She admires the snow flocked flowers
They last till she gets to the door
Softly, she will lay them down
To rest in snow once more

For Now

We're sad
It's time to say good-bye
You're gone and now we cry
And we will ever miss you
Our time
Is not our own to choose
We have numbered days to use
And all of life's things we must do
And then
Our earthly life will end
The Lord's will cannot bend
And someday we will come too
You rest
Until we meet again
For now, we'll remember when
You loved us. We loved you too

It's Material

Lace curtains
On two legs
You can see through them
They can't hide much
I have little use for them
I prefer moral fabric

Funny Feeling

You believe
You have hope
You have faith
A deep feeling of foreboding
Gives you unrest
That feeling is God
He's working a work
He always works for your best
Don't be disheartened
Or let a worry stay
Help get this work done
Do your part and pray

She Crossed the White Line

She sold her soul for the fine white lines
Disgracing herself as her smile declines
The grip on her soul, tightened each high
As her mind told normalcy good-bye

The lines, now her brains, dictated her plans
She begged, stole or borrowed to see the white lines
When no money availed for her high, she cried
When she looked up, she saw the sign
Jesus saves
What's left to lose but pain and abuse
The voice that answered the call, reached out
The words he spoke, and the help he sent
She knew there was a God, she had no doubt

Jesus helped her cross the white lines that day
She wouldn't see those lines anymore
Jesus saves, and she found that was true
She's stronger than she's ever been before

Her favorite lines now, she finds in God's word
The most beautiful lines she's ever seen or heard

Flower Porn

Nancy loved her flowers
She called it flower porn
She loved planting showers of flowers
For her yard to adorn

Nancy was in love with flowers
She often had flowers on her mind
Looking at the flowers she passionately acquires
Helps her to unwind

Nancy was into flower porn
She would plant seeds or potted plants
She didn't need a man to make her happy
Only flowers were going to touch her pants

Standing in Awe

Purified by his blood
Now I stand
To accept a crown
From my savior's hand
Humbled to bow
My head for a crown
Humbled to bow
My head down
His grace strengthens
My knees to stand
For who can stand
In his presence

The Reverse Mirror

The face saw a mirror it wanted to break
A reverse truth mirror, what it showed was fake
The smart ones, who figured out what was true
They were being accused of having the wrong view
The ones doing wrong were in a constant fight
Trying to convince people that wrong was alright
Conspiracy theorists, they called the knowing
While the media opened flood gates for all the lies flowing
Those that were trying to make America great
Were now being accused of racism and hate
The liars tried to convince us that gas wasn't high
They wanted socialism, give it a try
The woke had pipe dreams of a generation with no genders
Sterilized humans eating tofu tenders
They must be smoking something bad in their bongs
Hating what's right and loving the wrongs
The brainwashing was working on those watching fake news
The truthers found kindred souls, we shared the trues
The face wondered how much more people could take
Lies being truth and truth being called fake
The face said it's time to break the reverse mirror glass
Shatter it with truth and show the declass
Those that know God are the ones who can see
The liars are soon to be bent over God's knee

Frosting Flowers

Poor and unloved, she felt neglected
She didn't own anything to treasure
Being unloved, brings on an emptiness
Dreaming of cake was a rare small pleasure

She dreamed of cakes with frosting flowers
Something most people took for granted
Where there is no love, there is a pain
Where there was no love, frosting flowers were planted

Beautiful cakes, looked like a dream
Beautifully decorated cakes, she could feel love
It didn't matter, daydreams or night dreams
Frosting flowers were what she dreamed of

Now she is grown with her own bakery
She remembers the flowers from long before
She puts all of her love into decorating
Now she loves frosting flowers even more

No More Good Old Days

I miss the times when times were good
Kids played on the street in their neighborhood
Kids could ride bikes for hours and hours
Back then most people gave credence to God's powers
You could sit on the patio and drink a beer
You left windows and doors unlocked without fear
People loved to visit and laugh and tell jokes
Everyone stopped by to visit their folks
Kids liked to walk to the little local store
But there's no more good old days, not anymore

Now the windows are closed, and the doors are locked
The guns are loaded and some of them cocked
The kids can't play out on their own street
They might get shot when gang members meet
You can't let them walk to the local store
They might get kidnapped, raped or more
You wonder what happened, times use to be good
God's been evicted from the neighborhood

Kids used to learn and thrive at school
Now God's been expelled and there's no golden rule
Reading, writing, math, spelling, very little now
Brainwashing racism and genders, you wonder how
When you get rid of God, you get rid of good
There goes the schools and the neighborhood
People stopped believing in God and his powers
They've traded his laws for crime and gun showers
For those of us who love God, we're not afraid
We're watching them sleep in the beds that they made

It's all in God's love that these words are said
It's time to change the bedding and make a new bed

Beautiful Roses

When you see the elderly
When their walk slows
Their stature lowers
Their ears close
Their eyesight goes
Their pain no one knows
These are our treasures
Take care of those
In the garden of life
Our elders are roses
Some might have thorns
Or offend your noses
Keep them protected
Help them stand tall
When their canes lean
And their petals wilt and fall
A rose is still a rose after all

Cousins

My favorite cousins live a state away
I feel them living in my heart everyday
My childhood memories are here to stay
In my mind, in my heart
We're just a state apart
Though I feel like they're right down the way
In a car, it's a little far
By mail just a day
In my heart I feel like I saw them today

Crowns and Gowns

Honor the word and cleave to God
Hold on to his guiding rod
Stay the course and don't lay down
Keep adding jewels to your awaiting crown
The blood he shed, never stains
It covers your sins with no remains
Your righteous acts create your gown
A beautiful garment to wear with your crown

Mom and Dad

Sometimes when my mind sees mom
For a split second, I hear mom's voice
She was almost here, she felt so near
She would be, if it were my choice
My mind still sees dad at the kitchen table
His low growly voice hard to understand
I strain to hear, but I still feel him near
With his cigarette in his hand

I still see you, mom and dad
I make sure you're not forgotten
You are both gone, but your memory lives on
With love, from your number three begotten

She Lost Her Baby Boy

It was sad, she lost her baby boy
She lost her baby, she lost her joy
Her baby stopped breathing and now he's gone
She lives with a sadness, her grieving lives on
The death of a baby, how can you explain
When a mother is given this kind of pain
At times like this, what can you say
All you can do is pray
I've heard the saying, time heals all wounds
That may be true, but wounds leave scars
Some scars fade and some go away
Praying can help the ones that stay

The Cross Won

The needle doesn't sting anymore
The high is gone, it's not like before
The high was a trap; it was an evil trick
At first, the highs were beautiful from the needle prick
The highs that sent him to beautiful places
Have dwindled down to sickness and chases
Chasing money for drugs to feel well
Has turned into scoring or he feels like hell
How did the high ever get so low?
He hit rock bottom, no lower to go
There's no winning this one, he's at a loss
He said no more heroin, he reached for a cross
He held the cross in his hands and stared
He said "God please help me, I am so scared"
A feeling came over him he never felt before
God closed the window and opened a door
It was a battle to build a new floor
The cross fought the needle
The cross won the war

Granny Got Her Gun

Granny got her gun
She didn't put the bullets in it for fun
She said she needs to stand for her country
She's not going to let it be over run

Granny and gramps worked hard
They gave a lifetime of blood, sweat and tears
She wants to fight to reverse the damage
From the administrations last fifty years

Granny's watched the country she loves
Near stolen by socialist and communist rule
Now granny is feeling trigger happy
And I think that is pretty cool

She's never seen so much disrespect
For hard workers, America and the president
She said, "a China takeover isn't going to be fun'
Run commies run, cause granny's got her gun

The Dark Shift

The face went to the window and couldn't believe the scene
There was an enormous, evil, giant machine
It was working overtime to take America down
The crew leader was Satan, dressed as a clown
It happened in other countries as well
Satan was working to bring about hell
The machine had levers for every dis-order
Socialism, communism, Marxism, open border
It ran on cogs and pistons of lies
Trying to install a one world order in disguise
Satan had a crew, each with a button or lever
They conspired on their lunch breaks, they thought themselves clever
The products they manufactured, Satan's sales people tried to sell
They said their products were good, but they only brought hell
God is an expert when it comes to machines
He has his own crew who repairs and cleans
He's going to close the business and throw Satan out
God's crew will clean Satan's timeclock
And his monkey business, no doubt

Great Men

In the hallowed halls of God
Our great men live forever more
They cleaved to God with faithfulness
They served their country, some died in war
They protected our country in trying times
They lived the word and revered the cross
With honor they deserve, we will give thanks
For when they left earth, we felt the loss
Tried by fire they became pure gold
Barely could be found a thread of dross
They were God's powerful rolling stones
They rolled for God, never gathering moss

Stored Treasure

In a peaceful quiet town
He was living alone
No one remembers ever being in his house
There was no family known

He enjoyed helping his neighbors in town
People liked to have him around
He never felt sad or down
He had a confidence that did abound

He was alone but he wasn't lonely
He always let God lead his way
He lived his life for the one and only
He always made time to read and pray

One day, they found him passed away in his bed
They found his house was pretty bare
He only had two sets of clothes
Only one pair of shoes to wear

He didn't store his treasures on earth
To be corrupted by moths and dust
Most of his money helped the poor
Helping others, to him was a must

Now he's gone to his great reward
Heaven is where he stored his treasure
For the measure he used and doled out to others
God had greatly multiplied the measure

I feel an angel lived in town
If he wasn't one here, he is today
He showed us all, he lived for God
It's up to us where our treasures lay

Alan's Memorial

My brother has been gone for years
Last night I passed him in a dream
It was my brother's voice that asked
"Where are you going?"
"I'm going somewhere" as I stepped outside
"But no one knows I'm coming" I replied
I passed by him into the night
Though it was dark I saw the light
I know the light will come again
I know the light will prevail once more
Where I am going, I do not know
Down the street or far away
In the dark of night, I stood
I know the light will shine my way

I tried to show my brother the light
He lived in darkness, like the night
His breath stopped
His eyes closed
I hope in his last lucid moments
Dear God
I hope he saw the light
"Where are you going?" he asked
"I'm going somewhere" I replied in the night
"No one knows I'm coming"
But they will
When I shine my light
Alan...Can you see the light?

Flower in the Forest

There was a flower in the forest of trees
It longed to be like one of these
The flower hidden, the only one
It could not live without God's Son
Dear God "could I be like the trees"?
God said "no, you are not like these
I made you special from wind bourn seed
You are a flower that I need
The way you bloom and scent the air
I formed you with my special care
My trees are grand, but you are rare
You fought through more than you could bare
Every time you drop your seeds
You grow stronger in the weeds
Now bloom for me and show your worth
I put you here upon my earth
You are not a flower that no one sees
You are mine
I see you through the trees"

Grandma and Grandpa's House

We loved grandma and grandpa's house
As kids, we loved to run upstairs
Everything upstairs was old
To us kids, that stuff was gold
We looked in drawers and looked through books
We opened our uncle's door for looks
He had pennies laying everywhere
We got out quick to avoid a scare

Up and down the stairs we ran
As only little children can
We were ornery and deserved a yell
Maybe even a little hell
For tromping and stomping all over upstairs
Those were the days we had few cares

An old doll buggy and a cracked face doll
Was pushed between rooms, there was no hall
An old victrola with records to play
We cranked the handle and music gave way
Then down the stairs and out the door
On the farm, there was so much to explore
I so loved grandma and grandpa and their house
We all loved grandma and grandpa's house

Angel Nearby?

The horses in a group, standing together
They were all looking up to the sky
I don't see anything they might be seeing
Maybe there's an angel nearby
Maybe they all got the idea to fly
I didn't see a plane, even way up high
Or were they looking for rain?
You know, it's been so dry
I didn't see any birds, I know a hawk didn't cry
They just stood and looked to the sky
I looked too, and I thought, oh my
I hope it really was an angel nearby

Paul Parish

Paper carrier man, and part time cop
His little gray house, behind the Kwik shop
Rumored of what brought his birth
No purer soul, to meet on earth
A few whiskers on his face
Skinny legs and baggy shorts
A billy club on the bike he sports
When the sirens rang
He would peddle to the scene
He commanded respect
Though some were mean
I wish I was older and knew him better
But I was just a kid, so I'll write this letter

Dear Paul, I remember you
You were so pure and innocent
Through and through

You worked meager jobs
You did your best
In your old age, you dug graves
To put others to rest

If I could take a step back in time
You would be a special friend of mine
I would give you the respect that you deserved
You were one of God's servants and you really served
God's peace rest on you, Paul

Gem of a Friend

A friend is a friend until the end
I've heard some people say
Some friends come
Though most friends go
Not many ever stay
Acquaintances can fill a void
Some kind words when you see them
Though if you have a lifelong friend
You have a gem in a royal diadem

Talkie Walkie

They just met
It was love at first sight
She was good looking
He was alright
She talked for hours
He couldn't forget
She talked for hours
He was sorry they met
Sometimes some people
Look smart till they talk
She talked for hours
So, he took a walk

Along the Way

The good, the bad and the ugly
I think I've nearly seen it all
Along the way, at times I fell
Though I never did completely fall
I may have tripped and missed a step
I may have stubbed my toe on a stone
Along the path of life, I've found
God always caught me, I was never alone

Trees

You could walk through the trees alone
You could feel a presence towering you
You could feel God's breath blowing the leaves
If you love him the way that I do

I planted those trees, little bare root trees
I watered when dry, when it didn't rain
I kept the weeds and the grass mowed low
I like to walk through them, now and again

All of that hard work is now a stand of trees
Now my trees are mature and so am I
I planted them back when I could get on my knees
Now sometimes I walk through the trees and sigh

Some little trees just could not live
I would replace them to fill empty spaces
Just like parts of my life that died
I had to replant some things in other places

I look at the trees that barely grew fruit
I hope God doesn't see me as one of these
I hope I grew fruit or maybe gave shade
I tried to be one of God's trees

Now when I'm in the trees, I feel God
I feel a presence, when I'm walking through
The trees were my plantings and I'm a planting of God
We both like to see how our trees grew

Words

In conversations, hearts may touch
Words reveal what hearts conceal
As eyes are windows to the soul
Lips can keep or lose control

Bring it On

Life is calling
She must live
She feels she has
No more to give
Though when life calls
She hears the ring
To everyone
She's everything

She's God's, a wife
A mom, a boss
She reads the word
She lives the cross
Her hand she gave
She's now a wife
She gave birth
She nurtures life

She works to help
Her family live
After she gives all
There's more to give
Life is calling
The phone is ringing
Bring it on
She can handle the bringing

Looking for God

I went looking for God
I wanted to know what he wanted from me
I found a huge and glowing crowd
But there, God's words weren't free
I was too poor for the glowing crowd
The preacher's diamond rings, and he yelled so loud
They wore fine expensive clothes and fine expensive shoes
I only had clothes for everyday use
They were fill with righteousness
So much, it caused their heads to tilt back
I could see in their nostrils as they looked down at me
I felt they locked up God with their glowing money

So, I went looking again
I saw a sign that said mass at nine
This church didn't welcome walk-ins, that's fine
They had too many rules and too many stages
They always read the same words on the pages
I wasn't welcome to the body of Christ
They were a selfish church, and they weren't very nice

My journey didn't end there
I found some simple little churches

Some preachers weren't good teachers

Some read a scripture, then talked for an hour
When I left, I would be empty and feel a little sour
Some people were bossy running everything there
You'll find these little churches everywhere

So onward I did look
To learn the words in the book

Well, I found a chapel for everyday people
No fancy crowds or a selfish steeple
I saw a sign that said "All welcome here"
If you've said a few bad words, or liked to drink a beer
If you've had an occasion to tell a lie
You didn't mean to, but did to get by
If you did something bad because you didn't have money
Your redeemer is here, you are welcome here, honey

I said God I'm here for you
I found he was here for me too
I said I've been looking for your word to hear
He said, "I've been waiting for you, let's get started dear"
I'm learning chapter by chapter and verse by verse
Here, I'm not intimidated to open my purse
I'm at home in my Shepherd's Chapel

The Littered Countryside

The face looked with hate, at the giant wind towers
The turbines were installed but corrupt, greedy powers
One group wanted profits and shoved the crap through
The rest of us didn't want that junk in our view
Crooked commissioners catered to their plans
Now we are littered with giant turbine fans
Turbines litter the horizon, they produce little power
The greedy ones disregarded their neighbors for a tower
Turbines were tax deductions that made the corrupt wealthy
People who lived near them, many weren't healthy
Some people had headaches and didn't feel well
A constant buzzing made their lives living hell
God's poor birds, lying dead on the ground
As the turbine blades spun around
The face said these obsolete, toxin filled towers
Are going to be ended by coming higher powers
Free energy and new powers are almost at hand
Tax deductions will end, and broken turbines will stand
It's coming, the shit is going to hit the turbine fan
Unwanted wind farms weren't part of God's plan

The Real Things

A dozen birds in the bird bath bathing
Horses standing around a foal sleeping
Timely, beautiful rain when the ground is dry
These are the things my heart likes keeping
Some peoples' humor that makes me laugh
A stream of barn swallows flying when I mow
Corn husks blowing across the road in the fall
The winter glitter sparkles on top of the snow
Decorating my rock garden with big metal flowers
Bird houses and feeders put out here and there
When the sprinkler is going, it looks like bird heaven
That's when I don't have a single care
My macaw that sits on me and wants to be loved
Days that are so beautiful, I need to be out
All of the things that keep my mind off of politics
The real things in life and what it's really about

Midge

She put her ketchup in the freezer
She put her shampoo in the fridge
Her dirty clothes are in the dryer
Our sweet darling, darling Midge
She wore her coat to get her groceries
It's hot outside here, it's July
She misplaced her cart she filled with food
Went home and made a green bean pie

She's the kindest, sweetest lady
Our whole town cares for her these days
But don't you try to steal her money
She knows where her 38 special lays
Midge, we know old age has changed you
But please don't wear clothes made for teens
Honey, you're just a little too old
To wear those ripped, low-rise blue jeans

Midge, so huggable and cherished
We can't imagine no more you
It was you who brought us all together
To help you through the things you do
We'll visit you and drink your tea
It's strangely sweet though somewhat good
But no more pork'n beans in cookies
Chocolate chips please, if you would

True Love

He felt the silky maiden's hair
He fondly found his attention hers
The softness of her gentle voice
Discerning feelings that she stirs
Though no maiden he was seeking
Hearts and heartstrings intertwining
He forever more was hers
He would be her sun, and she, his shining

God's Cup

Let's give President Trump some love
He deserves it for what he's been through
When God asked Trump if he would clean up the mess
Trump told God, "I'll do anything for you"
The mess was deep, the rot was steep
Trump enlisted patriots to help clean it up
When America is clean and wearing God's sheen
All the patriots will get a sip from God's cup

Queen Melania

She should be queen Melania
Though not her title, she doth show
The virtuous qualities of so named
Queen Melania, your people bestow
Our first lady over our states
Your beauty surpasses all before
Your grace usurps any other seen
You should be queen forever more
Blessings also to King Donald
God anointed to clean up the mess
Queen Melania, please love our man good
He deserves it with all the mess and the stress
(And don't forget the dirty lying press)

Helen

Helen belonged to God
You could tell by the way
She treated people
Always kind
With friendly words
To say
If I had a church
It would have a Helen steeple

I'll Just Be Me

I know who I am
No embellishments for me
Tie dye is enough
It makes me feel free
I don't need green hair
A streak of pink might be nice
Though I'll just keep my own hair
I'll follow my own advice
Everything pierced from eyebrows below
I don't need piercings to show I'm cool
I'll keep my holes where they belong
I'm older and kind of old school
No desire for tattoos on my skin
I know where I've been, and I'll keep that within
Though there is one tattoo that gives me a high
King of kings and Lord of lords
God inscribed it on Christ's thigh

The Crop

I gaze upon the field of grain
I sense the toil to bring it through
With hope we'll have no storms with hail
As it near needs a harvest crew

The fields are ready to reap and shave
Men will again spend time and toil
To bring a bountiful harvest to bear
To give attendance to next year's soil

The crops are reaped and trucked or stored
The loads to town are weighed for price
Prices are paid, be it good or not so
The first tenth always goes to Christ
Another to wives if they are nice

The Visit

The face looked out to revisit the other faces
Most of them gone now, they found their places
They had to fight at school boards, teachers unions and our borders
Others were fighting socialism's sick disorders
Some covertly exposed evil with hidden tape recorders
Those of us left, we had other special orders
We were the ones who stayed home to pray
To back up the others who were on their way
The only way this face knew how to fight
Was to show the wrongs with a pen that could write
Writing the wrongs and giving them flare
Airing the grievances God called me to air
All those in the windows smiled and waved
We knew there was a new road of truth being paved
It would take us to a far better land
A place where lies and corruption have no place to stand
The face turned around and walked away
There was more work to do
And prayers to pray

God Loves Puzzles

God sees his hurting people
The many broken and shattered lives
They all have puzzle pieces to handle and join
Through everything bad, still love survives
God's love is everlasting for you
His love puts puzzle pieces together like glue
His mercy is unyielding and just as deep
He makes promises he will always keep
God helps with the borders, helping set the frame
He'll help with the center when you call his name
You can try pieces to find the right fit
You'll see God's hand when you say "that's it"
God blesses the pieces you put together
He protects them in the storms you weather
With his loving patience for pieces to try
He'll never leave or forsake you, so don't cry
God's plan can see the whole picture for you
Oops! This piece didn't fit, here's another one for you
Only a couple left, and you will get through
Even when done, it may need a little glue
When your puzzle is done, and you've found your way
Thank God who helped you along the way

Old Photographs

You can feel the toil
From long ago
In photographs
The past years show
Their faces wear their souls
To see
Life was hard
But they were free

Reaping Dill

It's so very true, you reap what you sow
I planted some dill and did it ever grow
It's in the garden, it's in the flowers
I like dill but it towers my flowers
It's in the grass, it's by the shed
I'm swimming in dill, it's over my head
The dill heads are pretty, the bees like it too
And I do love the smell,
Though I only use a few

Hand in Hand

As they walked, he took her hand
He felt her hand, his feelings stirred
He felt an overwhelming to speak
But he found not a word
As they walked, when he took her hand
She felt his strength and thoughts gave way
She felt an overwhelming desire to speak
But found no words to say
They were walking hand in hand
At times their arms would touch or brush
They both felt an overwhelming desire to kiss
Though, there was no hurry, there was no rush
Walking hand in hand, he squeezed her hand
He looked at her face and he saw her blush
They both leaned in a little closer to kiss
But it didn't happen, that made his face flush

Raindrops in a Drought

In times when your hoping seems endless
Wanting and waiting, want to give out
The only flood gates flowing for you
A few raindrops in a drought
Your hope is barely hanging on
You just keep hoping, that's all you can do
You wait and hope and want and then nope
There's rarely a sprinkle for you
These few sprinkles barely help with life's dust
You keep praying and holding hope tight
Endlessly waiting for clouds holding blessings
God's healing rain, and I'll be alright

Raindrops in a drought
Dear Lord, you know I'm keeping my hope
It's all in your timing, right now would be fine
I'm nearing the end of my rope
Hoping and praying with faithfulness staying
Knowing in your heart, it's God's will, not ours
God knows the right time to send his blessings
In his timing, he'll send you showers

Dr. Kraft

I think Dr Kraft the dentist was a sadist
I think he enjoyed kids feeling pain
He would drill your teeth till your eyeballs poured tears
He'd say, "mother, we won't use any Novocain"
Dr. Kraft talked with a pleasant soft voice
He'd say "mother, no Novocain will save you five dollars"
Next, he closed the door, so mothers couldn't hear hollers
He would stuff your mouth and begin with the pain
He said "don't eat candy and we won't do this again"
He once pulled my tooth without any numbing
He did it all the while smiling and humming
I came out of his office with my eyes full of tears
I still have memories of those childhood fears
Dr Kraft, I hope you didn't torment me for fun
I was glad when my mother said your practice was done

The Temple

Your body is the temple of God
Mine resembles a big old shed
I wish mine was a tabernacle
I'll get one of those when I'm dead
My temple needs a little repair
Some shored up studs and a smaller frame
Though the temple papers are safe and sound
As well as my heart that bears God's name

The Road Home

I walk the road alone
I'm not leaving a cloud of dust
I'm just going at my own speed
Some of my joints are wearing rust
I'll just walk and look around
I'll find something to catch my eye
I'll take in everything I see
Some dying trees or a field of rye
Wildflowers, that bloom in July
The birds, I love to watch them fly
Suddenly, I think oh my
I'm getting old, I'm going to die
For a split second my heart did race
But I'm going to the most glorious place
The most beautiful sights eyes can behold
They're waiting for me, when I'm done being old
I will be walking on streets of pure gold
Instead of gravel on a dusty road

Keep America Great

We're so sorry you're not happy here
Living in the USA
Our patriot hearts are just breaking for you
We can help you feel better today
We'll help you pack; we'll buy you a ticket
We'll even drive you to your plane
Now, let's get busy and find you a country
Where you can rightly complain
How about Venezuela, where you can starve
Or Cuba, where you could be killed
Maybe you could go to Iran or Iraq
Where your complaining can be fulfilled
Then again maybe communist China
Would allow you to be their slave
They can harvest your body parts
If you refuse to submit or behave
We could fill planes with USA haters
We can send you all on your way
We could bring back people from those countries
Who would really love to stay

We have an organization called GO
That's an abbreviation for Get Out
Pass the word to your like-minded friends
We would love to find them a route
When you leave, we will have a party, a big party
We will celebrate our great USA
Just a reminder, these are one-way tickets
Now, let's get you out today

The Horizon

It's just on the horizon
I can see it. Can you see?
Our countries are living under God
The people are free
We will be glad to see everyone's faces
No more false divisions between the races
Our countries and our people will prosper and grow
We will do it all together and we will know
Where we go one, we go all
God's people rose when the heard the call
Everyone gave all that they could give
To make our dream on the horizon live

The Journey

The journey, the less traveled road
Fewer souls, quiet days
Beauty lines the peaceful path
Lined with God's words and his ways
God's promises, like guiding signs
They show where I must go
As the destination nears
With relief, I see the glow

The Love is Alive

The face in the window, gave all control
To God, to a heart, to the pen and the soul
There is a love so deep, you feel it can't be reached
Then it comes alive to breathe
It comes alive to teach
Love is alive and gives life to a soul
Who struggled to live and have any control
The mystery is alive! The mystery is alive!
That's what happens, with God's love you survive
His love is like water that keeps filling a well
It replenishes itself and nurtures every cell
When you give it away, it will come back to stay
It's alive, love is alive, and it finds its way

God's love is alive, and his love covers me
Like the frost that flocks every twig on a tree
When God's light shines, there is glitter to see
That is how beautiful his love can be

When you give your love to God, it comes back to stay
Love just keeps growing, so give your love away
His love is alive and always finds a way
To return to the giver who gave it away
Love is alive

Birds Talk

In the forest of trees
Birds talk as they please
The owl wants to tell you of unknown things
Wisdom, they say, is what he brings
He said he listens to the birds as they sing
He said I can tell you this one thing
Our country has been on a downhill slide
We're turning, get ready for an uphill ride

An eagle told me he will have to fly higher
To make room for all the wealth we will acquire
The birds sitting on wires will deliver good news
They can hear everything on the wires they use
The vultures said they wanted to peck out the eyes
Of the evil traitors who found their demise
They wanted to peck the eyes right out of their heads
But you have a custom of burying the dead
They'll just keep looking for any more stink
We'll peck out their eyes, they said with a wink

The owl said the hawks were crying real tears
So grateful for God's people who ended the bad years
The birds voices carried to tell God the matter
From where they nested, they heard all the chatter
Glory to God who broke the snare

That's what the birds sang, flying through the air
All the birds of the earth and the forest
All sang together when it was time for the chorus
Even the trees of the forest were swaying
While the birds were singing
And for the words the owl was saying
The evil ones had no more evil displaying
Our great country and its laws, the people were obeying

Birds on a wire are a valuable thing
If you can understand what they say
When they sing

Grain of Truth

In a field over run with wild words
One seed was dropped, and something grew
When that one dropped its head of grain
It did as all other seeds do
Now it's a patch that thrives and lives
It's spreading fast and growing strong
It was making such a healthy patch
That none of the wild words could belong
There was no poison that could stop the growing
The beautiful patch was overflowing
Every time it grew and spread
Wild words were choked and now they're dead
You see, it was a grain of truth
When sown, it spread to make a stand
Those words grew to gain more ground
In time it was truth that covered the land

The Good-bye

The face in the window is saying good-bye
Some things the face saw, the face wondered why
The given messages the ears of the face heard
The pen in the hand, then wrote it to word
Times will come and times will go
The end time is something no one can know
It's time for our country to prosper and grow
Debts will be paid, and we'll see a glow
Then evil will rise in the guise of a man
He will come to deceive as many as he can
Be not deceived or fall for his lies
He will not be Jesus, but Satan in disguise
God's word says he is no respecter of persons
It was God, it was he who created us all
When the time is right to harvest the figs
Some will stand for God, many for Satan will fall
It was my duty to serve God's throne
God's warning advice for these troubled times
God had messages, he wanted me to share
Even though they were in the form of rhymes

The face in the window, looked out to see
The garage, some birdhouses and a white birch tree

Daydreaming

Dear fire, could you burn ever slower
I can daydream watching flames
I escape to thoughts I should not
While I am watching fire's games
Jumping flames and flickering
Embers glow like memories
Then the embers cool and die
While memories do as they please
Now the embers burn and glow
They beg for several logs of wood
I'll stoke the fire and end my daydreams
And face reality as I should